Coping with

THE BEAUTY MYTH

A GUIDE FOR REAL GIRLS

Stefanie Iris Weiss

The Rosen Publishing Group, Inc.
New York

To my sisters: May you grow to know yourselves well enough to see that you are beautiful beyond reason. Mirrors reveal nothing. Look within.

Published in 2000, 2003 by The Rosen Publishing Group, Inc.
29 East 21st Street, New York, NY 10010

Revised Edition 2003

Cover photo © IndexStock

Library of Congress Cataloging-in-Publication Data

Weiss, Stefanie Iris
Coping with the beauty myth: a guide for real girls / Stefanie Iris Weiss.
    p. cm. — (Coping)
Includes bibliographical references and index.
ISBN 0-8239-3757-7
1. Teenage girls—Health and Hygiene—Juvenile literature.
2. Beauty, Personal—Juvenile literature. 3. Self-esteem in adolescence—Juvenile literature. 4. Self-perception in adolescence—Juvenile literature. 4. Teenage girls—Psychology—Juvenile literature. [1. Health. 2. Grooming. 3. Beauty, personal. 4. Self-perception. 5. Self-esteem.]
I. Title. II. Series.
RA777.25 .W45 2000
155.5'33—dc21
99-059122

Manufactured in the United States of America

Contents

Introduction

Young women all over the world grow up believing that their very lives are dependent on how they look. The color of their hair, the shape of their bodies, and the surface of their skin can be as important as their minds and hearts. Girls are taught that they will be happy only if they are beautiful. We learn this deceptive lesson from our parents and teachers, from the media, and from Hollywood stars.

I wrote this book because of my own struggle down the path of understanding the true nature of the "beauty myth." In my early twenties, I began to realize that no matter how successful I was, no matter how good my relationships were, and no matter how my life seemed to those on the outside, I still carried around the angst that comes with feeling not pretty enough. No matter how many times I'd been assured by family and friends that I was indeed a "pretty girl," I still encountered images every day that made me feel inadequate. These images, in magazines and on the sides of buses, made me feel ugly. I began to talk to my friends and colleagues about this issue in a very different way than I ever had before. Rather than focusing on how unattractive I felt from the inside out, I began to think about why I and so many other young women I knew felt the way we did.

I read a book by a woman named Naomi Wolf called *The Beauty Myth*. It opened my eyes to the carefully constructed tactics of the beauty industry—the companies that sell makeup, clothing, and hair products to women and girls everywhere. I began searching for more and more lessons about beauty, culture, and low self-esteem suffered by most teens living in the Western world. I learned that millions of us living with bulimia, anorexia, body dysmorphic disorder, self-mutilation, and depression could find a way out of our misery by opening our eyes.

It is well documented that girls act like the strong and powerful people they are until they turn twelve or thirteen. Suddenly we start to talk less, look down at our feet, hunch over, and avert our eyes. Why do we do this? We want to be liked, of course. Who doesn't? Often we react this way because of what we believe are the expectations of the boys we want to like us. One of the purposes of this book is to prove that real girls are far more complex and beautiful than the kinds of girls and women they think are the male ideal—those on television and in the movies. Girls can mature into aggressive, smart, and real young women. And the endless energy expended by girls in pursuit of male approval as a symbol of love is simply a waste of time. It's a fact that girls love themselves better when they are creative. The companies that sell makeup and clothing and even teen movies would prefer girls to spend their time and especially their dollars by devoting themselves entirely to looking great to get guys. This is a standard so entrenched in society that it's hard to really wrap your brain around. It's with us every day, like the air that we breathe. As we move through the process of understanding beauty culture, it will all make sense.

Many adult models are made to look like twelve-year-old girls with very large, fake breasts. Their bodies are unnaturally thin and devoid of the curviness that is natural to women's bodies. Interestingly, female models are referred to as "girls" even when they are adults. This is an industry term. Sometimes images of emaciated models can work on the unconscious mind of a real twelve-year-old girl and make her feel like there's no good reason to grow up. She might secretly believe that if she stays as thin as she is at twelve, she will receive fame and fortune and happiness. Aren't all models happy? In the pages of magazines, helped by airbrushing and glamorous clothes, they sure look happy. But the answer is a resounding no.

Girls from different cultures and classes have to deal with different kinds of pressure to be beautiful. African American, Native American, Latina, and Asian girls living in the United States are doubly hit with the pain of beauty expectations. Images tell them that beautiful is almost always white. These girls have to deal with the racism of images idealizing white women and with the beauty standards of their own cultures. Young white girls have a different, but equally difficult, mountain to climb.

The truth is that the longer we accept the myth, the farther we will be from the happiness we deserve. We sometimes just let our obsessions with being pretty and "right" get in the way of all the great stuff we can do. And the thing is, it's really not our fault. This book will provide you with the tools you need to look at the world of beauty in a totally new way. It will teach you how to really be yourself, in all your true brilliance. It will show you how to allow your inner beauty, which is a very real force, to shine out and catch the eye of everyone that passes. It's time to shatter the mirror that says we're not good enough. We're more than good enough. It's time everyone around us found out about it.

One note before we begin: This is a workbook. As you read, have with you a journal or just some paper and a pen. (Some colored pencils or crayons will be necessary later on as well.) If you don't feel like writing as you read, reading this book can still be a deep journey. It might be an even richer experience if you get a notebook or even a cool journal from a bookstore and make it your own. Making your own journal from scratch can be a very potent start to confronting your issues with beauty. As you create your journal with paint, crayons, pastels, or collage, you will be making something truly beautiful. Before you start chapter 1, write a few pages in your journal about why you're reading this book and what you hope to gain from experiencing it.

What Is the Beauty Myth?

The evil queen in the fairy tale of Snow White and the Seven Dwarves stood before her magic mirror and implored it to answer one question: "Who is the fairest one of all?" Why do you think that was what she wanted to know?

I know I have spent many hours of my life before many mirrors asking why I couldn't just look a little better. I've made pledges to anonymous gods asking for mercy: "If only you'll erase this zit I'll never ask for anything else." "If I could lose just ten pounds everything would be perfect." The list goes on. I never really thought I was comparing myself to anything concrete; I just kind of knew that I wasn't good enough.

The pain of wandering in this space of longing for release from feeling ugly finally made me wake up and ask a new question: Who decided that I had to measure up to an ideal created by someone else? As a white, Jewish woman growing up in the suburbs of New York City, my ideal vacillated between a ridiculously tall Barbie figure (the wider cultural model of perfection) and a perfectly manicured, petite brunette (this was the local Long Island aesthetic). I am short and blond, so I could never win.

9

At the heart of the beauty myth is the fact that we believe we are engaged in a battle. It often makes us feel jealous of other women and girls, and strangers whom we deem more beautiful than ourselves. The part of this raging war that's actually ironic is that the girl you might think has it all is often feeling the same self-doubt you feel. Why do you think anorexia and bulimia are so prevalent across the world? Often "pretty" girls stop eating to try to literally disappear because they are so tired from waging war. It's a war that can't be won because the moment you find the perfect outfit, lose ten pounds, get plastic surgery, or otherwise alter your appearance, you'll likely find something new to hate about yourself. This attachment to our ego is a very important psychological concept, and we'll come back to it in a few chapters. For now, we need to concentrate on where and why we developed our current concept of beauty.

In our culture, the ideal female is thin, tall, white, and blond. Small nose, long, shiny hair, hairless limbs, big breasts, full lips, wide-set eyes, and flawless skin are thought to be close to perfect. (Many other cultures value very different visions of beauty, but we'll discuss that later.) So if you're black, Latina, Asian, a Pacific Islander, or mixed, you're almost immediately out of the running for meeting the ideal. If you're short or even slightly overweight, or if you have a big nose, acne, or any body hair, you probably already know what it feels like to be uncomfortable in your own skin. Imagine what it would be like not to think about how you look. Wouldn't you have more time to think about who you are? Wouldn't you have more time to just hang out?

The beauty myth has spread like a rumor. The idea that women should look only one way is as valid as saying the moon is made of cheese. Women are all different, and most women look nothing like they think they should look. Models in fashion magazines and actresses on television are the smallest minority. They also have tons of time and money to invest in their appearance. And airbrushing makes models look more like drawings than real women. Many models admit that they have eating disorders. This is tolerated in the modeling industry because industry leaders believe that the image of the rail-thin, leggy model is absolutely necessary to maintain. Fashion designers and editors at high-fashion magazines insist that the average woman wants to look at images of impossibly skinny models. This has been found to be absolutely false. We need to discover who sets the standards and why. Soon you'll understand why the beauty myth is a lot more connected to economics than it is to attractiveness.

People like Britney Spears and Christina Aguilera perpetuate the notion that we, as women and girls, are not living, or looking, up to standard. It's still really hard to go far in the music industry unless you meet Western culture's beauty ideal. Even Courtney Love, a self-proclaimed feminist, has had plastic surgery to "enhance" her appearance. She made her nose smaller, had her breasts lifted, and is often alarmingly skinny. Can you think of more than five currently successful female musicians who aren't skinny? And who aren't given a hard time about it? And aside from Rosie O'Donnell, Roseanne, and Camryn Manheim, there are rarely any full-figured women on television.

It's the images our culture presents that provide us with an understanding of who we are. Sometimes the real role models in our lives, like mothers, teachers, and older sisters, can intercede and protect us from the beauty myth. Often those who love us will try to explain that it's what's inside that's most important. But sadly, talk doesn't help much. There are those rare instances when girls will emerge from adolescence knowing that it's okay not to look like the perceived ideal. Often, all the good sense in the world can't get inside the minds and hearts of girls who are drowning in false images of beauty that destroy their self-concept. Images can go underneath the radar screen of thought and directly into the unconscious mind. Our media says that our culture values youth, beauty, and success. Often these principles are presented in the same package. Sometimes it's hard to tell them apart when we watch commercials and videos, read magazines, and look at billboards. Images have a way of burrowing into souls. We don't understand them with our minds. Rather, we feel them as we feel joy or pain. Have you ever looked at a painting or at the setting sun and felt the way it feels to be in love or the way it feels to be left by someone you love? This is why images are so powerful and why artists continue to attempt to commit their hearts to canvas.

Image Makers

If there are indeed what we could call "image makers," men and women who make conscious choices about fashion and appearance in our culture, how did they get that job? They are not evil people twirling their collective mustaches in boardrooms thinking of how they can work to destroy the self-confidence of young women. They are people in various industries like film, fashion, publishing, music, and television that stick to the status quo. But the fact that they fail to counteract damaging images is damning enough. If you're not part of the solution, then you're part of the problem.

Naomi Wolf says that "the beauty backlash against feminism is not a conspiracy, but a million separate individual reflexes . . . that coalesce into a national mood weighing women down; the backlash is all the more oppressive because the source of the suffocation is so diffuse as to be almost invisible."

The reason it has taken so long for women (and men) to critique the myth is that it's mostly hidden. It's a war that is fought inside the heads of women and girls, rather than a war fought openly. We fight against who we're born to be, whatever color, shape, or size we are. The battle scars end up directly on our bodies—the literal scars of self-mutilation, the ravages of bulimia and anorexia, and the immune deficiencies of those who use drugs or alcohol to cover up the pain of self-hatred.

It's important to remember as we go along learning about how to love ourselves that we are rediscovering the meaning of the word "beauty." This book is not written against the idea of beauty; rather, it has been written to help young women understand the true meaning of the word. Beauty, when imagined in an open way, can be a healing force in people's lives. It doesn't have to hurt. The poet John Keats wrote, "Beauty is truth, truth beauty." If we can look at someone and see her for who she really is, if her truth is visible, then she is beautiful, no matter what she looks like on the surface.

The philosopher Plato thought that beauty was "eternal" and "permanent." Our culture promises just the opposite. Beauty is imagined to be fleeting, something that we must cling to with all our might because at any moment it can be stolen from us. That's why a war waged within us with "beauty" at its source is such an effective tool. It keeps women and girls engaged. How will there be time for us to be out in the world competing with men for jobs and money if we must vigilantly fight against our ever-declining beauty? It comes back to each of us secretly begging the mirror for a miracle. Like the queen in the fairy tale, we believe that our worlds will be permanently damaged if we are not beautiful. How can we possibly be liked, let alone do well in school or get a good job, if no one wants to look at us?

Individuals have to break the cycle in their own hearts before the world will change. Internal change is revolutionary. It doesn't necessarily happen overnight, but study and reflection and even counseling can change your life and your self-concept. Once you understand the origin of the beauty myth, it will be easier to observe billboards and videos with some distance and a critical eye. The pain won't go deep into your cells screaming, "I'm not good enough!" because you don't look like an advertisement.

A good way to start thinking about which images make you feel least loved is to make a list of the ones that are most influential to you. Take out a piece of paper and try to write down ten images that have affected your understanding of the way women should look. Start with the one that has affected you the most. Write down the names on the left side of the paper. On the right side of the paper, write the whys.

Say you chose Madonna as your number one image. On the right side next to her name, write how she has influenced your concept of beauty. It could be something like "Because she wears really cool clothes from all over the world" or "Because she has a great body" or even "Because she's a great businesswoman and has a lot of power." Write whatever comes to your mind.

Now, on a second piece of paper, do the same thing, but use people from your own life, such as your mom, sisters, friends, or teachers. Write why you think they are beautiful and how they have influenced your idea of beauty. If your idea of beauty is really sophisticated and you understand that external beauty is far less meaningful than what's inside, try to step for a moment into the shoes of someone who is gripped by the beauty myth. Meditate on your concept of external beauty. We'll move on to our ideas of internal beauty in a little while.

What did you come up with? Did you learn anything about yourself and your concept of physical appearance? Do the people you chose look anything like you? Do you attempt to emulate them in the way you dress and style your hair? Next time you get dressed in the morning, think for a moment about who you are trying to be.

As you move through your life in the next few days, try to be aware of your judgments of beauty. As you look at people on the street, as you watch television, as you look at your teachers, as you hang out with your friends, observe your thoughts. A profound lesson taught by many spiritual traditions is that every judgment we make about others is truly a judgment about ourselves. So the next time you see someone in the hall and you secretly think

"Ugh, what terrible hair," or some other negative thought, you are really condemning yourself. And when you observe someone that you deem more beautiful than yourself, you are giving that individual a power over you that is not real at all. It's important to remember that all the secret judgments you make in your head will come back to haunt you. If you are standing somewhere and thinking nasty, depressing thoughts of yourself or someone else, you will likely appear angry and unapproachable. Who wants that? Not that there isn't a time and place for anger. It's more than okay to get angry at the institutions that perpetuate the beauty myth.

After you complete the lists, write a few pages about what it felt like to think about those you consider beautiful. Did you feel jealousy, anger, fear, rage, or satisfaction? Whatever came up for you is okay. Don't judge yourself for "bad" feelings. All our emotions are valid. Try to explore the levels of each emotion. Think of emotions like songs. They have a rhythm, a melody, and a tempo. There are some that are fast and furious, and some that are slow ballads. We need to pay attention to each of them. Our connection to what we consider beautiful is sure to inspire masterpieces of thought and criticism from our deepest selves. Allow yourself the space to explore what happens in your head and your heart as you think about what is beautiful. Soon you'll have more perspective, and it will make a whole lot more sense.

Who Created the Beauty Myth?

The beauty myth tells a story: The quality called "beauty" objectively and universally exists. Women must want to embody it and men must want to possess women who embody it.

—Naomi Wolf, *The Beauty Myth*

It wasn't always like this. Women have not always been victims of beauty culture. In terms of human history, the idea that women should be valued for their looks above all else is rather new. There are many resources that can expose you to a more definitive history if you're interested, but for the purposes of this book we're going to condense a lot of information.

HIStory

You may be thinking, "Why in the world would I want to know about the history of beauty culture when I'm suffering right now?" That's a good question. Why bother looking at history? How can it help us solve dilemmas of the present? There are many answers, but the first is that examining history prevents us from making the same mistakes over and over again. Sometimes we study and we continue to make mistakes, though. It's not foolproof. Often history is told from a particular perspective, to serve a limited worldview espoused by a limited amount of people. Sometimes we take it for granted when we read our history textbooks in school that all the information is accurate. Facts are funny things. They look different depending on who is observing them.

Look at the word "history": HIS STORY. By exploring the connections between our beauty and our culture, we follow many women and girls that have started the process of writing HER STORY. This is often a sad story, a tale detailing oppression and pain and struggle. But it needs to be told over and over. It will take a while for us to fill in all the gaps created by omission and suppression.

HERstory

It starts thousands and thousands of years ago, before the biblical era. This was a time before monotheistic religions existed. (Monotheistic religions worship a single god.) Many people were nomadic, and they worshiped many different forms of deities, or gods and goddesses. Goddess worship was a primary form of spirituality. Women were considered divine and were worshiped as such.

From about 25,000 BC until about 700 BC the Goddess reigned supreme. She went by many names—Ishtar, Isis, Venus, Aphrodite, Kali, and so on. The Divine Feminine was a potent force in many cultures. Some scholars speculate that the force was so strong that it caused a backlash that became what we call patriarchy, the domination and

18

control of the world by institutions that favor men. This doesn't mean that individual men control the world (although in most cases, it is individual men that run many of the powerful institutions that guide our lives). Rather, it means that the social world tends to be created with the benefit of men in mind.

"Patriarchy" is a loosely defined term. It is often used to describe the historical era that began when the goddess began to be replaced by male-identified gods. Once the patriarchy began to develop, women's roles changed drastically. They began to be depicted not as objects of worship to be serviced by men, but rather as objects of desire to be controlled by men.

Most of our ideas about beauty have evolved from the patriarchal era. Patriarchy is marked by a division of power that puts one group in a dominant position. For thousands of years in the Western world, the beneficiaries of the patriarchal ideal have been white men.

Economic Slavery

As agriculture developed, the idea of ownership of land eventually translated into the ownership of human beings, usually women. Even up until the late 1800s, there were laws in the United States that said that women were considered the property of their husbands. Still today, in some Muslim cultures, women are veiled because their beauty is considered such a temptation to men that it is dangerous for them to be exposed. (This is only one theory of the veil, however, and there are Muslim women that disagree with this notion.)

Chastity Versus Expulsion

This brings us to a strong theme in history and beauty culture. At some point, beauty began to be associated with chastity. Virginity and youth became the true arbiters of beauty consciousness. In Christianity, Mary, mother of Jesus, was held up as an icon, and all women were expected to live up to her example. Anything associated with the body and sexuality began to symbolize evil and danger in the world. Carnality (the physical rather than the spiritual or rational side of human nature) began to be associated with women at this time as well. But this was carnality not as a celebration of the womb, as it had been understood during the era of the Goddess, but rather as dirty and dangerous.

In pagan times, women were associated with the mystical darkness of the moon and the seasons of the earth. By the dawn of the Christian era, women could walk no middle ground: If they were not virginal and chaste, they were condemned as harlots. In modern psychological terms, this is known as the Madonna/whore complex. Men and boys continue to suffer its effects. If women cannot be owned and maintained like cars or pets, they are considered sluts and demons and called ugly names. There is a very good reason that the stereotype about boys liking only sluts or "good girls" still persists. We are still stuck in this ancient cultural morass.

Did you ever think about why there are so many negative slang terms for female genitalia? Our culture is still stuck in a consciousness where a woman's body is considered dirty, evil, and dangerous. See if you can come up with a list of words that describe a woman's body in a positive way. Compare your list with the words you may have heard used to describe women's bodies on television and in the movies.

20

An Economy of Ownership

As the Western nations moved toward a system of capitalism, the Christian Mary grew more and more virtuous as an ideal of perfect virginity and the quiet and respectful wife and daughter. The quality that best described Mary was passivity. Women needed to be passive vessels that were steadfast and there for their husbands. If a woman failed to display these "virtuous" characteristics, she would likely be unable to fend for herself. She would be pushed out of the market for attaining a husband. The concept of single motherhood (unless the father of one's child was literally God) was unheard of. Women who did not marry or had children out of wedlock were outcasts doomed to poverty.

Competing Costumes

What is the difference between the beauty myth of the Middle Ages of European culture and the beauty myth of China or of ancient Greece? History proves that fashions change with the winds. What is fabulous one day is out the next. That's what keeps women in line, constantly competing in a contest they can never win. A catalog of the fashions of just the last ten years proves this.

There have been different beauty standards in different cultures throughout history. Women who were forced to wear corsets certainly endured a painful beauty myth of their time, the Victorian era. Here we will focus on the middle-class, American beauty myth and how it has evolved into the beauty industry we live with today. Before the 1830s, the myth as we know it today could not have existed. This is partly because the first photographs were made at this time.

Before the mid-1800s, there were no mass-produced images, and middle-class women mostly worked alongside men. They needed to be shrewd, strong, and fertile, not necessarily pretty. The marriage market depended more on a woman's ability to raise a family than it did on her external beauty. But women still had to conform to the rules of chastity or they would be ruined for marriage.

As the industrial revolution progressed, the middle class expanded and families got smaller. Capitalism jumped on the bandwagon of domesticity, and the concept of advertising was created. This was the start of the contemporary beauty myth. A "cult of domesticity" developed. The glory heaped on virginal women was now heaped on women who perfected the art of homemaking. The ideal woman was one who knew how to raise children, make clothing, cook for her family, and keep a pristine home.

In the early 1960s, a woman named Betty Friedan wrote a book called *The Feminine Mystique*. This book served to open the eyes of thousands of women all over the country who felt trapped in their domestic lives. Like the character Nora in Henrik Ibsen's classic play *A Doll's House*, countless women woke up to their needs and sought work outside of the home. The backlash they suffered from this was huge. Unlike the working women of the 1940s, who went to work for their country during World War II, the working women of the 1960s were frowned upon. This time period (after *Mystique* was published) is often referred to as the second wave of feminism. The first wave of feminism was the era that climaxed with suffragists winning the right to vote for all women. We're in the third wave now, but we'll get to that in a few chapters.

The Barbie Era

For more than a century, women had become more and more enmeshed in the idea of the ideal woman they witnessed over and over in advertisements everywhere. Hollywood films emerged, and the bombshell was born. A perfect home still took slight precedence over a perfect body and face, but both of these needs competed with one another to keep women busy. Barbie, the ultimate expression of our society's ideal woman, was born in 1959. If Barbie were a real woman, she would have a forty-two-inch bust, an eighteen-inch waist, and thirty-three-inch hips. An average woman has a thirty-five-inch bust, a twenty-nine-inch waist, and thirty-seven-and-a-half-inch hips. (Today over 90 percent of girls ages three to eleven own a Barbie doll.) Can you imagine what this image did to countless young women who were taught to believe Barbie was perfect? Did you ever own a Barbie doll? What do you remember about it? Write in your journal about what Barbie means to you.

After *The Feminine Mystique* was published and the prison that women inhabited in their private homes was revealed, women began to work outside of the home in large numbers. They began to acquire their own money, and with this, a little bit of freedom. As Naomi Wolf explains it, the beauty myth we know today emerged when women were just about to break free of the chains of domesticity. The balance of power was about to be tipped, and the industries that keep the engine of capitalism running responded by creating the beauty myth. Advertising and the modeling industry boomed at this

Barbie Doll

This girlchild was born as usual
and presented dolls that did pee-pee
and miniature GE stoves and irons
and wee lipsticks the color of cherry candy.
Then in the magic of puberty, a classmate said:
You have a great big nose and fat legs.
She was healthy, tested intelligent,
possessed strong arms and back,
abundant sexual drive and manual dexterity.
She went to and fro apologizing.
Everyone saw a fat nose on thick legs.
She was advised to play coy,
exhorted to come on hearty,
exercise, diet, smile and wheedle.
Her good nature wore out
like a fan belt.
So she cut off her nose and her legs
and offered them up.
In the casket displayed on satin she lay
with the undertaker's cosmetics painted on,
a turned-up putty nose,
dressed in a pink and white nightie.
Doesn't she look pretty? everyone said.
Consummation at last.
To every woman a happy ending.

—Marge Piercy

time. A model named Twiggy, the first borderline anorexic role model for women, became the first supermodel. Women were on display more and more: in ads, in films, on television, just about everywhere. Since that time, the modeling, fashion, and cosmetics industries have taken on lives of their own. They account for much of the advertising we see on television every day.

What do you think the girl in the poem "Barbie Doll" went through to achieve acceptance? Have you ever felt as if you had to modify your face and body to please the people in your life? What do you think the poet is trying to tell us?

Naomi Wolf compares the beauty myth to an ancient German torture device called the iron maiden. It was a coffinlike box with a beautiful woman painted on the outside. Victims would be locked inside to either suffocate or be impaled on stakes. This is what women suffer at the hands of the beauty myth: On the outside, all appears glossy and wonderful. On the inside, the pain is unbearable.

Ask yourself once again how much of your life is spent thinking about how you measure up. Do you believe that you're a victim of the beauty myth? When you look in the mirror, do you see yourself as you really are? Or do you see someone who is missing something?

There is a theory about the way women experience themselves in their daily lives. John Berger, a British art critic and historian, wrote a book in the 1970s called *Ways of Seeing*. It is essentially a book about images and how they affect us. In it he writes, "One might simplify this by saying: Men act and women appear. Men look at women. Women watch themselves being looked at. This determines not only most relations between men and women but also the relation of women to themselves. The surveyor of woman in herself is male: the surveyed female. Thus she turns herself into an object and, most particularly, an object of vision: a sight."

This is sometimes referred to as the "male gaze." When you look in the mirror, rather than seeing yourself there, you see yourself as you would imagine yourself to be appraised by men. This doesn't mean you are judging yourself by the standards of a boy that you like necessarily, although this happens a million times a day. (Remember that lesbians can suffer from the male gaze as well.) It just means that because the standards for beauty are ideals created by and for men, women are judged by the male "surveyor" inside themselves.

Breaking down the male gaze is a tough task. It takes a deep understanding of all the levels of self-judgment that have existed throughout your life. It means sifting through what you believe you like and finding out what you really like. Very often you'll surprise yourself as you move through the process. Right now, write a few pages in your journal from the perspective of the male surveyor inside of you. What does he expect of you? How does he think you should look? Can you catch up with his ideal? What are the alternatives?

Who Decides How We Should Look?

A quick flip through any current women's and/or teen girls' magazine will reveal a series of photos of women who fit the standards for beauty in our culture. Even when the editors attempt to print stories that reflect real issues in girls' lives, the photos on the facing pages never match up. Real-girl stories are still pretty rare. There are a few magazines that are more likely to print them, but we'll deal with that in more detail later on. More often, popular magazines print articles with titles such as:

- "Wake Up with Perfect Hair"

- "Win a Wardrobe Makeover"

- "Back-to-School Boy Guide"

- "Reel Him In and Get Ready for Love"

- "Fall's Gotta-Have-It Fashion"

These titles are a random sampling of articles from any fall issues of various teen magazines over the last five years. What do they say to you? What we read is supposed to reflect who we are and what we care about. If the writers and editors of these magazines know so much about us, why do they believe all we care about is our hair?

Perhaps there is something more complicated going on. I doubt that the folks who make the magazines we read truly believe that all teen girls care about is the way they look. And I really don't think that they are evil. We'll come back to the content of the articles in teen magazines in a little bit. For now, let's look at the ads the magazines contain.

The truth is, the only way for magazines to make money is through advertising dollars. Let's look at how advertising works. Companies produce products. They've laid out money in the production process, and their goal is to make a profit. How do they get the products to consumers? Through advertising, of course.

Ads come in many forms. There are billboards, television commercials, Internet banners, ads in newspapers and magazines, and so on. The bigger cosmetics companies have entire divisions devoted to advertising. Other companies hire independent firms to advertise for them. They spend millions of dollars a year researching what they think people will spend their hard-earned money on. They use focus groups, telemarketing, and direct mail surveys to get their information. Obviously it pays off for them, or they wouldn't invest the time or the money. Cosmetics companies fiercely compete with one another to win the disposable income of consumers everywhere. Right now, teens are the hottest consumers, and they are being courted by everyone in the corporate world.

Let's look even deeper into the beauty industry. Take a moment to look at your medicine cabinet. Take out the products one by one and think about which of them you really need. Think about the moment that you bought a particular cosmetic, or "health and beauty aid." Did you go to the store looking for that particular product because of an ad you saw? Did you decide on your own that you needed it and should seek it out? Were you walking around and saw the product on the shelf and bought it spontaneously?

A recent look into my own cabinet revealed dozens of products that I haven't used in years. Some of them I used once but never threw out because I thought that perhaps I'd need them at some point in the future. Hair spray, leave-in hair conditioner, mousse, gel, sculpting spray, tinting cream—the list goes on and on, and that's just the hair list. I often wonder what I'd be able to buy with all the money I've wasted on hair products and makeup in the last ten years of my life. I could probably afford a new notebook computer, something I truly need, if I hadn't wasted all that money. But that's another story!

So back to your cabinet. Have you found anything interesting yet? Think about your morning ritual. What do you do when you wake up and hit the bathroom? We can all agree that a toothbrush, toothpaste, floss, and soap are necessities. That's just good hygiene. And if you wear contacts, you need solution, of course. What else do you do besides brush and wash? How long does it take you to get ready? Just some stuff to think about.

Many women are convinced that they need three or four separate kinds of moisturizers each day. Eye cream, throat

29

cream, regular face cream for the day, and often an alpha-hydroxy antiwrinkle cream for nighttime. People generally use another kind of cream for the body, one for hands, and, very popular recently, one for the feet. Women have been convinced that aging is evil, and a good majority of them have bought into the idea that special creams and lotions will save them. What ideas have you bought into about teenage skin? Think about your cleansing ritual. Do you use soap, toner, and moisturizer? Have you learned the "steps" of a particular product's cleansing line? Think for a moment about how strange it is that we sometimes believe the promises of these products.

↪ "Your face has over 20,000 pores. Smooth, even skin starts with smaller-looking pores." This is taken from a soap ad. Okay, let's run to the store because the soap company apparently has the answer to all life's problems: perfect skin. Ads promise us that if we buy particular products, our dreams will come true. They play on our fears of being cast out, of being left loveless.

↪ "If the emotion fits, wear it! Anything goes in the wardrobe of life and we're ready to try it on. We may not get it right the first time, but hey, we're in no hurry, we're girls." This is an ad from a cosmetics company. It essentially says that our emotions are simple things that we can try on at will. This ad implies that girls are hyperemotional, flirty, playful, pretty, crazy, empty headed, and moody. And the fragment, "We're in no hurry, we're girls," says that we have nothing better to do than apply nail polish and perfume.

↪ "Your skin is as individual as your fingerprint. The freshest, healthiest look possible demands precise skin care, uniquely effective for your skin." This copy is from an ad for a skin-care line. It also says that it took "eight years of scientific research and clinical studies" to formulate this line of products. Citing dermatologists is another way that cosmetics companies try to sell products. In small print at the bottom of the ad, it says that this research was conducted by an "independent research center based in Paris and funded by [the cosmetics company that produces the product]." What I want to know is how can this research center possibly be independent if it is funded by the cosmetics company? Companies don't invest their capital in endeavors that won't eventually bring them profit. Realistically, the "research center" is an R & D (research and development) facility, not a good-will-for-the-world's-skin laboratory. It exists to create the products the company will sell. The people who create the ads must convince the people who read the ads that they need the products. If you've been living your whole life without them so far and you are okay, why do you need them all of a sudden? This is the kind of question to ask yourself when you start to fall under the spell of an ad.

Psychological Manipulations

Advertisers know a lot about human psychology. In fact, an informal poll of advertising executives reveals that many of them studied psychology in college. Why do they need to understand the human psyche so well? Advertisers seek to understand our motivations. If they believe that catering to particular fears or desires will sell a product, they will use that information to get inside our heads. They use the same techniques that screenwriters and directors use to manipulate audiences into getting scared, crying, or laughing. No matter what ad copy says, there are very few products out there that are created because of the benevolence of their producers. The primary goal of every producer of goods is one thing: profit. They will do whatever it takes to empty your wallet.

In the late nineteenth century, women routinely died from the ingredients in cosmetics. Some face lightening powders contained arsenic, or rat poison. More recently, the quest for perfection has led many women to die from complications of silicone breast implants. The late nineteenth century was the era in which advertising dawned. Because images could be much more easily disseminated, thousands of upper middle-class women fell prey to their charms. "Ladies guides," precursors to contemporary women's fashion magazines, were published. Several decades later, all classes of women began to be exposed to the lies and manipulations of the cosmetics industry.

Retouching

One interesting thing about fashion magazines is that the standard created for normal women and girls in the shape of models is even less real than it appears on paper. While we gaze at pictures of women we believe are "perfect," we don't realize that graphic designers have worked them over just as makeup artists have. Almost all photos in magazines are retouched. This means that any skin imperfections are erased away. Cellulite vanishes. Dark circles under the eyes are lightened. Designers can even slice inches off model's thighs with their sophisticated computer software. It makes young women everywhere want to look like cartoons: images that don't even exist. Even the models can't live up to the standard created by the industry.

Fashion trends have as much staying power as a feather in a windstorm. Since the end of the conservative Victorian era, women's sexuality has shown in their clothes. Corsets, which arrived in the late 1800s, constricted women's bodies into the desired shape: small waisted, large breasted, and slim hipped. Women often fainted and saw doctors for crushed organs because of tightly closed corsets. The girdle was a later version of the corset that appeared in the 1950s, the era of the blond bombshell. Marilyn Monroe and Jane Russell were the pinup girls who represented this ideal. (The current incarnation of the girdle is called innerwear, essentially a seamless girdle made of Lycra.) In the late sixties, the model named Twiggy came on the scene. She weighed ninety-two pounds. The thin ideal has not changed much since. There are a few magazines that cater to the full-figured woman, but that's it. But for a whole world of women, the irony is that their shape is deemed "full-bodied" (which is an ugly word in the fashion industry) and the tiny percentage of women who are shaped like models are considered the norm. Doesn't that seem backward to you?

It's important to note that teen girls have been making their own statements about how they should look for a long time now. Society has become far less strict about personal fashion choices. When not in the corporate world or in another institution requiring uniforms (like the army or a Catholic school), people can get away with wearing just about whatever they want without getting into official trouble for it. The trouble we perceive in our minds is wrought by the images we consume.

Since the early 1990s, more and more young people have been taking risks with fashion by getting pierced and tattooed. Now these activities are beyond trendy; they are the mainstream. It is a strange moment for the fashion world because street kids are way beyond the elite designers who decide how they should look. For years, they have been sending trendspotters out into some of the cooler neighborhoods, such as New York's Lower East Side, to track down the next trend. One such trend that the fashion world is caught up in recently is "hippie chic." Copies of the vintage bell bottoms available in thrift stores for under ten dollars are being sold in designer shops for upwards of five hundred dollars. The insanity continues.

But all of this doesn't affect the beauty standard for women very much, though. Although we are liberated from corsets and girdles, we are still stuck in the vise of having to stay thin and beautiful. This is a standard that never seems to change. We are allowed to take more risks with the way we choose to adorn ourselves, but we continue to make ourselves literally sick in order to conform to the beauty standard. In most high schools across the country, girls are struggling in secret against the idea that they are missing something. Ads promise us that if we can just hide that imperfection, our lives will change miraculously. No more acne, and I'll get a boyfriend and my broken self-esteem will be repaired. If I buy that hair spray, maybe I'll get a part in the play and then my grades will improve and I'll get into college. When you stop to think about it, it doesn't make sense.

Image Domination

Our world is dominated by images. Television and film play a far larger role in the lives of those coming of age in the new millennium than it did even twenty years ago. We live in a visually ruled universe. Billboards loom large over our cities and small towns. Televisions are everywhere we go, even in school, and they seem to be always on. It seems we live half our lives online.

There is a definite downside to technological revolution. Teens today seem to be a lot more plugged in to the entertainment industry than kids were a couple of generations ago. Some teens are so involved in the lives of the celebrities they like that they forget that they don't really know them. Television talk shows have made knowing the personal details of strangers' lives commonplace. It's impossible to escape violent television images, no matter where you live. Because we swim in images in this culture, it's often hard to separate our own lives from what we see on the screen. It makes it harder to rely on real-life role models, like mothers and older sisters and good teachers. They aren't on television, so they don't seem to be that important in the scheme of things. Let's look for a moment at who is on television and why.

The majority of women on television are very young, very thin, and meet the beauty standards of our culture. On MTV, for instance, you rarely see an overweight or "imperfect"-looking woman or girl. The famous women who don't exactly fit the standard get mauled by people like Jay Leno every night. Janet Reno, a high-ranking official in President Bill Clinton's cabinet, was constantly harangued by male comedians during her tenure. *Saturday Night Live* often shows sketches of famous women and exaggerates their beauty and weight flaws for comedic effect. Star Jones, one of the co-hosts on the show *The View*, is regularly mocked because she is a large woman. The list goes on, and there is a consistent pattern. Is this nice? Is this something to be proud of?

Women who come close to meeting the standard and are in the music, film, or television industries have a tough path to tread. There is vicious pressure in these industries to look a certain way. Actresses are often turned away because they're not the right "type," regardless of their talent. They get the message that says it doesn't matter who you are as long as you look good.

The case of the rumors surrounding Britney Spears is an interesting example of this dynamic at work. There is much speculation about her breasts. Many people believe that she has had implants. If this is the case, it's a very sad situation. To feel pressured to enlarge one's breasts as a teenager because it will help one's career must be pretty scary. On the other hand, if her breasts have grown naturally, isn't it horrible to have the public make a big issue out of it?

Sex Sells

There is an old adage in the entertainment industry that says, "sex sells." But sex seems mostly to mean naked and half-naked female bodies everywhere. Shows like *Temptation Island* and *Baywatch* featured women in bikinis acting incredibly stupid and little else. *Baywatch* was considered by many to be mostly devoid of plot, with terrible acting and sloppy directing. But it was one of the most popular shows of all time. Why? Because young, thin, large-breasted women ran up and down the beach on every episode.

The nude female body is on display everywhere in our culture. The female body is a beautiful thing. By objectifying it, however, ads diminish women as thinking, feeling human beings. Remember when we discussed the idea of the male gaze in the last chapter? Most of the images we experience of women on television, in films, and in advertising are projected at us from the perspective of the observer/man. If more women created videos, television shows, and films, perhaps the women visible to us would look more like real women. Perhaps females would appear less as objects to be used and more as subjects to be studied for their potential achievements in the world.

Consequences of the Myth: Hurting Our Bodies

Eventually the negative emotions we carry in our bodies turn into disease. Stress becomes a headache. Fear becomes an ulcer. And self-loathing becomes anorexia, bulimia, body dysmorphic disorder, self-mutilation, and a myriad of other diseases. The beauty standard can make us sicker than we ever imagined.

What do you consider to be your ideal weight? Do you weigh yourself regularly? Is shopping for clothes a painful experience because you can't fit into the size you want to? It is apparent that body shape and size are an obsession in our culture. Open any magazine or turn on the television and you are assaulted with advertisements for weight-loss products, exercise videos, and health clubs. Thin and toned bodies abound, and they are not on view because they're healthy. They are flaunted because they appear to meet the ideal beauty standard. If strong bodies were on view as the ideal because of what they do instead of how they look, the epidemic of eating disorders might decline significantly.

In 1995, the Centers for Disease Control reported that 11 million women had eating disorders. Just about everyone knows someone suffering from an eating disorder or has suffered herself. Boys get eating disorders as well, but the numbers are not as high. Anorexia and bulimia have had their share of media attention, including books, news reports, and after-school movies. But other eating disorders, like binge eating disorder and run-of-the-mill compulsive dieting, for instance, remain in the closet. In our culture, a woman's compulsive focus on the size of her body is considered normal.

Seven- and eight-year-old girls are suffering from eating disorders. This was unheard of even a decade ago. Most eating disorders start with dieting. A girl who wants, for instance, to rid herself of "baby fat" will go on a fad diet, not realizing that most fad diets are dangerous and rarely work. She'll eat a severely limited amount of calories for a few weeks and lose a few pounds. After she ends her diet, the weight will inevitably come back. And the cycle will have begun. This isn't the only way that eating disorders begin, but it is a common start.

Types of Eating Disorders

Anorexia Nervosa

Anorexia nervosa is marked by starvation. Girls and women with anorexia severely restrict their food intake in an effort to lose weight. However, the weight loss quickly becomes dramatic and dangerous.

People with anorexia suffer intensely negative effects on their health. The effects of anorexia include weakness, fainting, headaches, constipation, growth of fine hair (lanugo) all over the body, and a yellowing of the palms and soles of the feet due to lack of nutrients. Bones become severely frail and can break easily. The body will begin to digest its own muscles and organs for energy because it is not gaining enough energy from food. A girl will stop having her menstrual period. Long-term effects of anorexia include infertility, heart irregularities, and kidney failure. Left untreated, anorexia can kill.

Even though anorexics are terrified of food, it rules their lives. Mealtime is traumatic, and many girls ritualize the event to make it easier to get through. They hide their food, spend a long time cutting it, chew for a long time, or don't eat at all.

Even when a girl with anorexia is severely underweight, she will look in the mirror and see a distorted image of her own body. She believes she is fat. Anorexia has other psychological consequences as well. Many anorexics are also clinically depressed and feel isolated from family and friends. Ironically, the effects of anorexia worsen this isolation. When starving, a girl will feel invincible, because eating is the only thing she feels she can control, and she will refuse the help of others.

Bulimia Nervosa

Bulimia nervosa is characterized by bingeing and purging. Bingeing is consuming a large amount of food in a short amount of time and feeling out of control while doing it. Usually this behavior is done in secret. Purging is eliminating food from the body, usually by throwing up right after a meal. Those who suffer from bulimia often consume large quantities of laxatives to purge the food from their bodies. The term "exercise-induced bulimia" identifies those who will binge and compulsively exercise in order to burn the calories.

Some symptoms of bulimia are uncontrollable eating and purging by vigorous exercise, vomiting, or abusing laxatives or diuretics. Like anorexics, those who suffer from bulimia suffer from a distorted body image. They see themselves as being overweight when they are usually of a normal weight. Unlike anorexia, bulimia does not cause severe weight loss. Most of the calories from food are already digested by the time a person purges. However, bulimia is still extremely dangerous for a person's physical and emotional health. Bulimia is usually accompanied by depression, mood swings, feeling out of control, swollen glands in the face and neck, heartburn, bloating, dental problems, irregular periods, constipation, indigestion, a sore throat, vomiting blood, weakness, exhaustion, and bloodshot eyes.

Binge Eating Disorder

Binge eating disorder is compulsive overeating without purging. It is usually done in secret and is almost always followed by feelings of guilt and shame. Food is used as a dysfunctional means of coping with emotional pain. Some of the symptoms of binge eating disorder are episodes of binge eating, eating when not physically hungry, frequent dieting, feeling unable to stop eating voluntarily, awareness that eating patterns are abnormal, weight fluctuations, depression, shame, antisocial behavior, and obesity.

What Causes an Eating Disorder?

There are many factors that precipitate eating disorders. Media images play a central role, but there are lots of other reasons. Not all of the reasons apply to everyone with an eating disorder.

Some girls want to hide in their bodies. They may be hiding from family problems, sexuality, social situations, and rejection. Losing a tremendous amount of weight is an almost literal way for these girls to become invisible. Another way to hide is through obesity. Being extremely overweight is a way of being invisible or hiding, too.

Sufferers of sexual abuse may overeat and become obese, to hide their bodies from the world because they are ashamed and blame themselves for the abuse. Psychologically, they feel that if they are fat and undesirable, no one will hurt them again. Food and fat become a kind of armor to keep emotional pain at bay. Another reason people develop eating disorders is because they feel out of control in their lives. By starving themselves, overeating, throwing up, or compulsively exercising, some girls feel that they can regain control over their emotions and their lives in general. Sometimes a girl's eating disorder becomes her only friend, the only thing she can relate to in the world.

It is important to remember that many girls who don't suffer from clinically defined anorexia or bulimia can suffer from eating disorders, too. Anyone who has gone on a diet when she didn't need it, felt guilty about eating, overexercised, or felt compulsive about her weight knows what it's like to start down the path to developing an eating disorder.

Our culture sanctions just about every behavior that has to do with losing weight or looking buff. It's hard to see how there can be anything wrong with working out or eating a little bit less food. The media is not fond of drawing distinctions between being fit and looking good. It's one thing to eat balanced, healthy meals to provide energy for working out and developing muscles to be strong. It's another to limit your food intake and work out because you believe that if you don't no one will love you. Working out becomes a problem when it becomes a compulsion.

How often do you think about what you eat? Do you ever feel guilty after eating something fatty or high in calories? How often do you exercise? If you don't exercise, how do you feel when you witness people working out? Do you feel guilty? Write about some of these questions in your journal. Choose the one that fits your lifestyle best. If none of them apply to you, just ask yourself how you feel about your body and what you feed it every day.

You need food to live. Think for a moment about the places in the world where starvation reigns, like certain parts of China and Africa. The people there would probably be shocked if they knew that people in the United States starved themselves on purpose. In Fiji, where Western television just arrived a few years ago, abundant flesh on women's bodies used to be a sign of beauty. Since television shows like *Melrose Place* have become popular there, the girls have started developing eating disorders! Images can do a lot of damage.

Other Kinds of Self-Torture

Self-Mutilation
Girls have created other troubling ways to deal with emotional pain in relation to the body. Self-mutilation has received a lot of attention in the last few years. Girls who

self-mutilate often suffer the same struggles as girls with eating disorders. They deal with their pain by cutting, burning, and otherwise mutilating their bodies. Self-mutilators claim that their emotional pain is lessened when they feel physical pain. They get an actual rush out of harming themselves. The sight of blood after cutting can feel like a release, but it is actually part of a vicious and painful cycle.

Body Dysmorphic Disorder

Body dysmorphic disorder is a disease characterized by an obsession with a perceived defect in physical appearance. This can be an actual slight imperfection or an imagined one. Sufferers of BDD believe they have imperfect noses, poor skin, strangely shaped eyes, and ugly breasts. The range of imperfections they believe they suffer is as wide as the body is complex, but the skin, hair, and nose are the most common targets. This disease is sometimes called imagined ugliness syndrome. People with BDD are so obsessed with their perceived imperfection that they cannot function in their normal lives.

Some BDD patients go from doctor to doctor searching for solutions. They sometimes attempt to have repeated plastic surgeries but are never satisfied with the outcomes. As a result, their lives are seriously ravaged.

Drug Abuse

Many teen girls turn to drugs and alcohol as a way to numb the pain in their lives. The effects of drugs and alcohol may temporarily blot out anxieties and make girls feel cool or part of a group. The problem with this, however, is that drug and alcohol use can take on a life of its own.

Imagine (or maybe you don't have to imagine) that you are feeling completely isolated and alone in life. If you're walking through the school parking lot and run into a group of kids, and one of them offers you a beer or a joint, would you accept it? It's tempting, huh? But guess what? Even if you make some new friends, you'll be putting yourself in serious danger.

Of course you know that it's illegal to drink or smoke if you are underage, and it's illegal to do drugs no matter what your age. Who knows, the risk of it may even appeal to you. But the real danger is that you're covering up your loneliness and letting it slide. When you numb your feelings, you leave yourself wide open for your private insecurities to multiply. And the teen years are when many young women not only experiment with drugs and alcohol but begin to slide into drug and alcohol addiction.

If You Think You Have a Problem

If you have a problem, you probably know it in your heart. Maybe someone in your life has tried to bring it up, and you just changed the subject because it was too hard to talk about. Maybe you've admitted that you have a problem, but you don't want to face how serious it is.

The first step to healing is to admit that you are suffering. People with eating disorders have a tremendous amount of guilt, and guilty, shameful feelings make it hard to talk about. Forgive yourself and know that you are not alone. In the Where to Go for Help section at the end of this book, you'll find a list of resources to help you deal with eating disorders.

If you think someone you know might have an eating disorder or another problem, try to first talk to an adult you trust about her illness. If you can't find anyone to share it with, gently direct your friend to the resources that you think will help her, like this book.

The Inner Killer

Girls in America are in great danger. Beyond the violence in our schools and on our streets, girls face an inner killer every day. It takes a whole lot of work to dump destructive attitudes, including culturally imposed standards of beauty that we have internalized. That's why it's so important to understand the history of women's oppression due to "lookism." We need to teach our little girls that it's more important to have a nimble mind than a shapely form, that true goodness doesn't grow from looking good, and that the heart is more important than its casing. If you were taught these lessons when you were a small child, would it have made a difference in the way you see yourself today?

Most of the women I know have endured some kind of eating disorder or serious crisis of self-esteem. I can't even remember all the moments I've sat across from one of my friends and listened to her list her imperfections. Almost always, the lists were full of items that I could not see. "I hate my hair, it's not full enough, straight enough, long enough, short enough, soft enough, red enough, blond enough, black enough . . ." Or "I hate my thighs, breasts, hips, stomach, calves, upper arms, waist . . ." Or "I hate my eyes, nose, lips, skin, hands, feet . . ."

I know that this kind of obsessing is not a sickness shared only by my friends. I hear it in ladies' rooms, locker rooms, cafes, and everywhere that women congregate. With each other, sometimes we feel comfortable enough to list our flaws, almost as if we are in competition with one another to be the ugliest. "No, I'm fatter than you. I so am!" my friends have told me. It's a deep, seemingly limitless pain we share in search of an elusive beauty standard. It is about the most basic of human emotions: love. We want it so much that we're willing to go to any length for approval. In our culture, we imagine we will be loved if we are pleasing to imaginary men. The media is a front for this invisible man we carry around behind our eyes. We look in the mirror and he stares back, criticizing us into submission. So we starve ourselves, cut ourselves, and sink into mental illness to escape from the pain.

Understanding the source of the pain and being able to intelligently criticize the beauty standard when it tries to slam us is the first step. If you feel you are a victim of any of the illnesses discussed in this chapter, remember that you are not alone. Millions of other women and girls are suffering, but healing can happen as soon as you let it. There is a whole slew of resources available to women everywhere, and with time and work, eating disorders and other body image disorders can be a thing of the past.

Being a Girl of Color in a White World

As we briefly explored in the first chapter, girls of color are doubly stung by the power of the beauty myth. They experience the pain of not meeting the culturally imposed white ideal, and then they must try to meet the standards of their own culture/color.

Although the civil rights movement is forty years old, racism is as virulent as ever. There are still racially motivated hate crimes reported in the news every day. In August 1999, a man went on a shooting spree in the Midwest, killing Orthodox Jews, Asians, and others he assumed to be from minority groups. Police routinely practice a form of institutionalized racism termed "racial profiling." They pull over members of minority groups on highways under the assumption that they are involved in criminal activities.

It seems that despite changes in school curricula, national and local government agendas, and a spirit of tolerance promoted by people seeking justice, we still see the effects of racism every day.

Similar to the legal changes brought about by feminism, like the right to vote and the right to legal abortion, the official strides of the civil rights movement have not eradicated everyday acts of violence and intolerance. Affirmative action has afforded people of color more access to institutions like colleges and corporations (although it has been overturned in several states in recent years, but that's another story). But it seems that the more successful non-whites become, the more they are feared by racists. This is a form of scapegoating, or blaming others for one's own sense of inadequacy.

White Feminism

Modern feminism, unfortunately, addressed only the needs of white women in its first incarnation. With its focus on middle-class, educated, and elite women, the wave of feminism inspired by Gloria Steinem and her colleagues implicitly overlooked women of color. There was no real critique of classism (intolerance of people based on their economic status or class) or racism, and no deep look into the lives of black women. This is changing slowly, and feminist scholars are beginning to look at different cultures and classes. Black feminists, like Audre Lorde, Angela Davis, and bell hooks, have helped to turn this around. But what does this have to do with beauty standards in the United States?

Young white girls playing with their first Barbie doll experience the pain and confusion of believing that Barbie is the ultimate, but impossible, woman. Young black, Latina, Asian, Native American, Pacific Islander, and other non-white girls see something completely alien when they look at dolls with white skin and blue eyes. Only in the last fifteen years or so have dolls been made to resemble other ethnicities than Caucasian.

Now, compound that emotion with the impact of the media—magazines, videos, news reports, and so on. Again, things are changing slowly, but the standard for beauty in our culture is still a lot closer to Gwyneth Paltrow than Lauryn Hill. This is beauty racism. When women of color do appear in magazines, they are often "exoticized," or otherwise made to look nothing like real women of color.

In the early 1980s Whoopi Goldberg created a performance art piece in which she played various characters. One of the characters was a young black girl, maybe five or six years old. She put a white T-shirt on her head, and in a cute little girl's voice, explained that it was her "long, luxurious blond hair." She personified the ache of not fitting in that so many black girls experience in a white world.

Cultural Stereotypes and the Media

Stereotypes of black women still abound. On soap operas, there is a sea of whiteness with one or two black characters, usually a couple. Prime-time television is segregated. Shows have either white or black casts. There are far more "white" shows than "black" shows. On the programs with mostly white casts, like *Friends, Frasier, Dawson's Creek, Will and Grace*, etc., one almost never witnesses a person of color. There are some shows, such as *The West Wing*, that have a mostly white cast with one black character within the core cast. Of the major news broadcasters, there have been a few people of color or from ethnic minorities throughout the years. Connie Chung, Bryant Gumbel, and

Al Roker are examples. But still, they are usually single entities in a mostly white cast of characters. In the fall of 1999, activists protested the lack of casts of color on the new slate of prime-time television shows. They organized a boycott of the major networks. Today, thanks to such boycotts, casts of television shows are starting to reflect the natural makeup of ethnic America.

Why are people of color so underrepresented? It certainly doesn't reflect the true racial balance of America. And what do these images do to young people of color? The answer is that it makes them feel invisible. As victims of anorexia and bulimia attempt to make themselves invisible because of shame, young girls of color are taught to hide their true selves. Many young women are offered solely images of white beauty. Imagine how hard it is for young girls of color in a white world who don't have personal role models to help them see their true selves. For them, the journey is even harder.

The Beauty Myth and Its Problems for African American Women

Within the black community, above and beyond the white beauty myth, young girls also must meet standards imposed by African American culture. The color issue is a huge and troubling force. Some people attach a stigma to skin color that they think is too light or too dark. There are skin-lightening creams that exist to change the appearance of the pigment in black skin. Since the black pride movements of the 1960s and 1970s, the drive toward lightening skin has diminished, but for girls of earlier generations, it was an obsession. Women and girls used skin bleaches with names like Nadinola, Covermark, Nevoline, Beauty Start, and Dr. Fred Palmer's Skin Whitener. Ads in magazines like *Ebony* promoted this type of product. Skin lighteners are still used today, but generally only to lighten dark patches of skin. Because acne was considered a "dirty" disease in the early part of the century, girls from disenfranchised groups felt extra pressure to have perfect skin. Acne was viewed as an indication of poor hygienic standards and poverty. For African American girls, acne was doubly difficult. Pomades were sold to improve dry skin, but they tended to clog the pores and cause a condition called pomade acne.

Many people believe that girls of color do not have body issues at all. Usually the only beauty issue widely acknowledged among African American girls is the ever-present hair debate. (We'll get to that in a moment.) A lot of folks think that because there is a perception that black men prefer heavier women, women and girls who are black don't desire to be thin the way that white girls tend to. And there probably is a little bit of truth to the idea that some black women feel more comfortable with ample hips and thighs. But eating disorders aren't just a problem for the white, middle-class segment of society.

Becky Thompson is the author of a book called *A Hunger So Wide and So Deep: A Multiracial View of Women's Eating Problems*. It details the lives of eighteen women of different races and their struggles with anorexia, bulimia, dieting, and compulsive eating. She found that many of the women she studied developed their eating disorders because of racism, sexism, and sexual abuse. It is hard for anyone with an eating disorder to talk about her problem and seek help, but it is doubly hard for girls of color. There is a shroud of silence in black communities regarding eating disorders. It is sometimes viewed as a "white girl's problem." For black girls with eating disorders, there is often an even deeper sense of shame.

How can girls of color who believe they have an eating disorder deal with it and keep their developing identities intact? The same rules apply as did in chapter 4. But understand that you can make your own rules and set up the parameters for healing. If you feel alone, like no one else in your community knows what you are going through, know that, sadly, there are many other girls just like you. Seek out a support group. There might be pain bottled up inside of you, but looking at it will help make it go away.

Hair and African American Women

Hair is a major issue for black women. Being born with what is considered "good" hair is often seen as a blessing. Many black women don't believe that they have "good" hair. Styling and setting the hair takes up energy. Some women spend many hours and many dollars having their hair braided or weaved. Others straighten their hair because they have internalized the idea that "nappy" hair isn't beautiful. What's most interesting about these cultural standards is that although they are not necessarily imposed by whites, they often move toward making black people look less African. Malcolm X tells a story in his autobiography of how he attempted to straighten his hair with lye and burnt his scalp severely. This was not uncommon.

Black hair is usually coarse hair, hair born of beautiful African roots. Are you at ease with the hair you were born with? What kinds of messages have your family and community given you about your hair? The media isn't much help here either: Most black women in the music industry and on television have super long tresses like Naomi Campbell or wear wigs like Star Jones. Lauryn Hill is a notable exception; she wears her hair *au naturel* and is proud of it. Wearing dreads, Afros, or natural hair is not favored in many circles.

How does your mom wear her hair? Some of my black friends have told me stories about their mothers who refused to leave the house on days when they couldn't get to the salon to get it styled. Getting microbraids (which can actually damage the hair and scalp) and weaving the hair are extremely common practices. Lots of other girls opt to straighten their curly tresses instead of braiding or weaving. This is another potentially dangerous practice, since it damages the hair. This is part of the fear of natural hair. Would you consider wearing a natural look? When you look at other women and girls with short hair, natural hair, dreadlocks, the hair they were born with, how does it make you feel?

Whatever your decision, remember that you are making the choice for yourself, not because someone is convincing you that you should change something fundamental about the nature of your appearance. There are always alternatives.

Finding Peace
Inside Our Bodies

Being a teen is rough for seemingly endless reasons. Emerging sexuality, changing peer relationships, school, parents, and the state of the world all collide and seem to land on your head. The beauty standard somehow keeps you busy worrying about the state of your body when you could be spending time on stuff that is a lot more important.

So how do we get to the stage where we care less about our reflections and more about our real role in the world? It takes work. It takes a whole new understanding of how we see ourselves and how we are seen. It takes compassion, empathy, and forgiveness.

When most people think of forgiveness, they assume that it is a gift to someone else. Sometimes forgiving ourselves is the most important apology we'll ever make. The first step is to forgive ourselves for all the mean things we have ever thought about our bodies. Take a moment and do this in your journal right now. Try to remember all the terrible thoughts you've had about who you are. Start like this:

Dear me,
I'm writing to tell you that I'm so deeply sorry for all the
things I may have said over the years that hurt you.

Then write down all the mean things you can think of that you have told yourself, even if you still believe that they're true. Think about what you've learned so far by reading this book and how forces outside yourself may have contributed to your damaged self-esteem, the reason for the negative "tape" going on and on in your head. Keep going. You may have a long list. Leave a few pages blank in this section of your journal, and when you remember more things you need to forgive yourself for, add them to the list.

A note: Because this is a self-help book, we are going through some of the steps that a trained therapist might go through if you went into his or her office for help. After you finish reading the book, you can decide whether or not you need more assistance to deal with your beauty issues than this book was able to provide.

Family Life

Next we have to explore our childhood. For many people, childhood is the rich wilderness mined to understand the pain of the present.

The media influences us tremendously, but the messages we receive from loved ones can have an even more staggering effect on our sense of self. Remember that our parents, grandparents, friends, sisters, brothers, and teachers have learned much of what they know about beauty from the media. Now that we understand the history of images a little better, perhaps we'll have more compassion for some of the messages given to us by our families. They live under the lens just as we do.

Childhood

Childhood is often a time of deep wounding. Some of us suffer the trauma of sexual abuse, physical and verbal abuse, or the loss of a parent. Some of us live in poverty, and some of us may live in relative material comfort, but with little or no love to keep us warm. Even those of us who haven't suffered a statistically common cultural wounding experienced the usual growing pains of journeying from childhood to adolescence. Many doctors believe that teenage anorexia is symbolic of a psychological fear of growing up. They theorize that girls stop eating so that they will literally stop growing up. This can indicate a fear of sexuality or a fear of adult responsibility. If children don't get the proper nurturing while they're small, they might not ever be ready to be adults.

Early Messages

Messages about beauty start when we are born. Girls are dressed in pink and given dolls and other "girly" toys to play with. Boys are encouraged to be aggressive. Girls are praised for being pretty. They learn at a very young age that beauty gets attention. Boys learn that acting out gets them attention. Some statistics have shown that teachers, male and female, pay more attention to the more attractive students. It has also been shown that teachers encourage boys to raise their hands and speak out in class, whereas girls are praised for precise handwriting more often than boys are. In fact, a book by authors Myra M. Sadker and David Sadker, *Failing at Fairness*, explores this issue in depth. Again, this shows how perfection and prettiness win points for little girls, showing them that this should be their primary goal.

Do you remember what it was like to be a little girl? What messages did you receive about how important it was to be pretty? All of us have had different experiences. Some of us received a tremendous amount of love and praise from our families and very little from the outside world. If you grew up feeling like you were outside of the boundaries of the beauty standard because you were over-weight, a minority, handicapped, or otherwise didn't fit in, your peers may have teased you and you may have been virtually ignored by your teachers. Maybe you did fit the standard of your community and the wider world, but your parents put so much stress on being attractive you thought you could never keep up. Maybe you fit the stan-dard so well that attention was never focused on anything other than your looks. That is the other side of the coin of the beauty myth. What was your experience?

Mothers

Our mothers are huge influences on how we see our-selves. As girls, we look at our moms as barometers of how to be a woman in the world. We watch the way they carry themselves, the way they relate to our dads and other men, and how they feel about their bodies. Often, just plain observation of our mothers teaches us a lot about self-esteem (or lack thereof).

I am lucky enough to have a strong, loving mother who is not overly body-conscious. When I was growing up, she did praise me for being pretty, but she also told me that I was smart, capable, creative, and powerful. My beauty issues have mainly been inherited from my grandmother, whose painful relationship with her mirror was handed down to me. I spent a lot of time in my grandmother's Brooklyn home because my mother worked full-time. My grandmother was smart, funny, and brave. But she was also obsessed with her appearance. I can only imagine the effect she might have had on the world had she not been constrained by an appearance obsession! We would liter-ally spend hours together while she sat at her makeup table, in a separate dressing area she had specially built for primping time. She had what seemed like thousands of bottles of creams and lotions. I would sit at her vanity when she was elsewhere and play make-believe. I imag-ined I was glamorous by smearing on red lipstick and try-ing to put on her false eyelashes. (Can you relate?)

She had three closets full of clothes, many of them unworn because she decided she didn't look good in them after she brought them home. Although I was about seven years old and was not capable of offering mature advice, Nanny would stand before the mirror with me and ask whether I thought she should get a nose job. She had wanted one her entire life but was afraid of surgery because her father had died from an operation when she was twelve. She would look at her profile and wince. She would call herself ugly. Her nose was prominent, but I found it beautiful. It comforted me and reminded me of the strength she was capable of sharing.

With company she always owned the room. But when we were alone together, I became her sounding board. It was as if she forgot that I was a young, impressionable little girl, and she was so deeply in pain that she needed to get it off her chest. I'm sure that this was all unconscious; she probably never thought of the mixed messages and the consequences of her words. Later in life she would obsess on her need for a face-lift and pull the skin up around her face to see what it would look like if she were younger. When she turned fifty-seven, she stopped telling us how old she was and joked that she was really twenty-five. It was clear that her fear of aging wasn't funny at all. After my grandfather died and she started dating again, she was embarrassed about what my mother's age would reveal about hers. Youth was beauty, and for my grandmother, life without beauty was hardly a life at all.

With hindsight and a lot of deep exploration, I've come to terms with how my grandmother's messages about beauty have scarred me and affected my relationship with my own mirror. When I was little, with blue eyes and blond hair that were rare in my family, my grandmother would question where I got my "Irish" nose. She would say, "Where did you get that nose, from the postman?" I could hear in her voice the fear and denial of her Jewish genes (although I'm sure I didn't interpret it intellectually at the time). She hated her nose because it reminded her that she didn't fit in as a Jew. She was terribly teased as a child because she was Jewish, and she was grateful to God that my small nose and blond hair would protect me from such an experience. I was teased for a lot of other reasons, but we'll get to that later.

Our parents and grandparents often transfer their own issues with beauty onto us. They don't do this on purpose, but their pain is often unresolved and they don't know how else to deal with it. That's a lot of responsibility for little girls to balance the images we absorb from the media in addition to the standards imposed by our families. It is common for dieting mothers to ration their daughters' intake of foods for fear that they'll become fat. Because they are so afraid of losing love to a thinner woman, they force their daughters to face the same demon.

Many anorexic girls are daughters of women who have eating disorders themselves. From friends and colleagues, I've discovered that women blame their mothers for much of what they feel about their own bodies. Mothers have encouraged their daughters not to leave the house without makeup. Mothers have forced daughters to get particular haircuts. Mothers in my hometown, believe it or not, have offered plastic surgery as a gift to their teenage daughters.

The other end of this extreme is the jealous mother syndrome. Even when our mothers love us fiercely and deeply, we might represent for them something they feel has slipped away in their own lives. They might even feel some rage toward us, but that's not something that can be easily acknowledged. A mother who has a deep fear of aging, inspired by the beauty standard, may watch her daughter mature sexually and feel jealous when she gets attention from men and boys. The mother might look at her daughter's body and feel fear and jealousy rather than pride.

You know how we discussed the issue of jealousy and hatred between strangers? That emotion is even more complex when it comes from a woman who is supposed to know, love, and care for you. So if a young girl is shopping, for instance, with her jealous mother, her mother might turn a deeply critical eye on her daughter as an unconscious defense mechanism against her own feelings. Rather than tell her daughter that she looks beautiful in whatever she puts on, a mother in this state might tell her daughter that she is too fat or too skinny, too sexy or not sexy enough, etc. This cutting down is a way of taking away her daughter's sexual power, the power that the beauty myth bestows in our culture. Try to stay aware of your mother's messages, conscious and unconscious. If you think this dynamic might exist between you and your mom, you can try talking to her directly about your feelings, but be prepared to release some strong emotions. Going to a professional therapist, together or separately, might help both of you with your issues a whole lot.

Fathers

Our relationships with our fathers are complex and often problematic. Many fathers dote on their daughters and call them "the prettiest girl in the world." They truly believe that their daughters are the most beautiful, and this is a point of pride with them. Unconsciously, daughters learn that the only way to get affection and attention from men is to be pretty.

Sometimes fathers don't know how to be comfortable around their developing daughters. When we hit the teen years, we naturally drift away from our parents, but the divide between dads and daughters sometimes feels as if it can never be bridged. It's a very uncomfortable issue, but our dads might feel weird about us because we are becoming women. They get funny about the idea of dating, wearing makeup, and the clothes we wear. On one hand, they might beam with pride because they think we're beautiful, but on the other, they might be afraid that as we grow up we'll grow away. They may become jealous of the boys we date. Of course, this scenario is more likely in a nuclear family, one where there is a mother figure and father figure living with the daughter.

Resolving the beauty issues you've inherited from your family can take time and insight, especially when you have to continue living in their home and dealing with issues that may continue to be unresolved for them. For me, it took leaving home and the distance of some years to come to terms with my family's beauty messages. You can start right now. In your journal, write about all of the people in your life and the beauty messages they've given you. Start with the women in your family: mother, stepmother, sisters, grandmothers, aunts. How much does your current concept of beauty relate to their influence? Next write about the men in your life: father, brothers, uncles, grandfathers. What kinds of messages did they provide you? Write as much as you want, and remember that you can come back to this section if you forget anything.

Life in School

The cultural climates of our schools also have a huge influence on how we believe we should look and who we think we are. I grew up in an affluent community, but my family was strictly middle class. We couldn't afford the fancy designer clothes that most of the kids in my school wore. I had play dates with kids whose entire wardrobe came from Bloomingdales and who got a bunch of new outfits every season.

At first I felt jealous and sad and wished my parents could afford to buy me what I wanted. I was teased by other kids in school because I would wear the same outfit more than once a week. Jordache jeans were hugely popular when I was in fifth grade, and I could only afford an imposter pair. Kids made fun of me for my "fake" jeans.

One of the benefits of this pain was that it made me search for my own, unique style. In high school, I started shopping at thrift stores, and it wasn't only cheap, it was cool! Eventually I gained the respect of my peers because I made the decision to look nothing like them. I took a chance on the beauty standard, and with a little creativity, I won.

Style

Styles come and go. We can get attached to a brand or a new fad because we see it on television or worn by someone popular. Chasing trends is like riding a hamster wheel: You'll never get anywhere. If you constantly buy what's being shown in fashion magazines, it's likely that you'll need to throw it out the following season. Or it will just fester in your closet like my grandmother's purchases did. It also wastes money. It will serve you much better if you try to know what you like best and what you feel comfortable in rather than relying on what everyone else decides is cool. If you truly think something trendy is cool and you can afford it, by all means get it. But try to note before you make the purchase if you are buying it to win approval by your peers. There's a big difference between expressing yourself with your style and dressing to impress others. It's a lot more gratifying to be yourself.

Adornment

What if you really like to dress up? There's nothing wrong with that. If you make getting dressed into an art form, you will be a step closer to extracting yourself from society's beauty standards. Since feminism was born, men and women have kept busy accusing feminists of being "antibeauty." There is a false notion that has permeated the culture that one cannot be strong, beautiful, and in control. When we stay stuck in conventional beauty routines and trendy styles, we are agreeing with these naysayers. Strong women and girls don't necessarily believe that creative style goes against the grain of our power. As long as we know that we are working to eradicate the world of patriarchal power ploys, we can and should put on whatever we want. That means that we can dress like vixens, gypsies, biker chicks, ravers, hippies, punks, or whatever else tickles our fancy and expresses our vision.

Adornment is used by every culture, ancient and new, to express the social climate and the needs of the individuals that inhabit it. Tribal tattooing is a traditional ritual in the Philippines. In Nigeria, a tribe called the Wodaabes are deeply concerned with male beauty. The men dress to please the women and even compete in beauty contests. Interestingly, the women of this tribe are the ones who possess the economic power. And the Western world has for centuries been obsessed with the "kept woman."

One way that we can take our power back is to appropriate ideas from the world of fashion and elsewhere, and make them our own. Appropriation is one of the most important tools you can put in your bag of insurgent tricks. Remember what Robin Hood did? He stole from the rich to give to the poor. When you appropriate an idea or a style or word, you take the meaning back from its possessors. The gay liberation movement has done a masterful job of taking back the power of words like "queer" and "fag." Queer was a slur used by homophobes for many, many years. When the movement started in the late sixties (coinciding with the black power and feminist movements), the pain of those words were turned around and appropriated by gays. You can appropriate ideas, too. It's a metaphorical way of wearing your politics on your sleeve. Think about the styles that have intrigued you. Why do you like what you like? Try to see underneath your desire to wear a particular fashion. Are you into it because you think it will win attention from guys? It's okay to want attention from people that you like. In fact, it's perfectly natural. What's not so natural is how we get caught in a consumerist maze hoping that clothing or makeup will set us free from loneliness.

Now make a list of all the ideas/words/tools/fashions you'd like to take back from oppressive groups. This does not have to be a list based on politics. It could be about teachers, parents, other kids in school, television stars, musicians, or anyone who you think influenced you to attach to their dream. Think about your own dream. Now imagine how you could take a piece of that idea back and make it into your own. What would you do? Write about it in your journal. If you can't think of anything right now, just write about what the new idea of appropriation means to you. Do you think you might be able to put it into use in your life? Do you think the people around you will get it? Does it matter if they get it?

Trying On Types

When I was a teenager, there were a lot of different groups to attach oneself to in order to make a statement about one's worldview. It blows my mind when I witness how many more exist for teens today. As a teacher at a New York City high school, I've seen wild creativity worn on the bodies of teens. There are punks, ravers, straight edgers, granolas (or Deadheads, if you prefer), hardcore kids, skate rats, preps, jocks, Rastas, homeboys, and on and on. There are also degrees of each. One can also exist in two or three groups at one time, depending on taste. Or someone can be a Deadhead for the first two years of high school, for instance, and then decide that he or she is more closely aligned with the jocks.

It's endless, but this kind of typing, which goes on in schools in small towns and large, is dangerous. The horrific school shootings that took place at Columbine High School in Colorado in the spring of 1999 attest to this. What if you don't fit into any of the above categories? Where will you feel safe, and with what company? What if you just haven't figured it out yet because you're still trying out lots of different ideas? There is a natural tendency for teens to try on many personalities until they figure out what to give their heart to and who they truly are. This trip differs for boys and girls. Because girls are trained to dedicate so much of their energy to attracting boys and being perfect, they can get lost and divorced from the true pleasure and fun of adornment. Learning to dress for yourself can take time and effort. But it's worth the work because every morning can be an art project for you. I'm not suggesting you spend an obscene amount of time getting ready for anything. They'll be plenty of days when you will roll out of bed and let sloppiness be your master. That's fine, too. In the end, you'll end up getting the right kind of attention from everyone around you. This will be based on intrigue and curiosity, and on your personality, not on your looks.

One note: Sometimes our parents might not be too psyched about our fashion and/or political choices. You know your parents best. If experimenting with style is going to cause a war in your house, talk to them first. If your parents are conservative and you already feel as though they don't understand you, tread this territory carefully. Rebellion is natural during the teen years, and many parents are braced for you to shock them. They might have a few tricks of their own in the bag, such as grounding you, telling you that you are weird for wanting to look different, and so forth.

Many kids dress differently in an unconscious attempt to thwart their parents' power over them. They wear exactly what they know will make their parents angry. They even get a kind of satisfaction from their anger. If you begin to experiment with fashion appropriation in an attempt to disentangle yourself from the beauty myth, you might want to clue your parents in so they don't freak out. This will show them that your behavior isn't an insult or rebellion against their parenting, but rather something that you just have to go through. Just like we forgave ourselves for the mean things we've told ourselves over the years, it also helps to forgive our parents for their own wounds. You can even show them this book and tell them about the journey that you're on now.

Moving Beyond the Body

So far we've explored the external traps that taunt and twist our inner selves. We've determined their source and discussed some of the actions we can take to distance ourselves from the pervasive images that choke our culture. In addition to opening our awareness and knowing that most of what we see has nothing to do with who we are, we can do some inner work that will help us deal with the damage that has already been done. Training the body and mind can help us stay stress-free and connected to our true selves every day.

Bridging the Mind and the Body

Yogis have known for thousands of years that the only way to still the mind is to master the body. When we obsess about our appearance or tell ourselves mean things about who we are and how we look, we hurt our inner selves. Sometimes it repeats in our brain like a broken record, and it makes us feel totally out of control. It becomes a kind of tape of the mind on continuous play.

We can begin to address this by taking approaches to bridging the body and mind. Mastery of our minds and bodies will bring us closer to the reality that we are not just our bodies; the body also encases the reality of our heart and soul. The art of movement takes you beyond the body by going through the body.

Traditional Exercise

Until fairly recently—the last fifty years or so—girls have been restricted in their participation in athletics in our culture. Even now, when little girls want to play, climb trees, and run, they are often told to do something safe or quiet, like play with dolls. However, that's changing more and more. Girls and women are taking sports to a new level.

Whether it is a solo sport, such as biking, weight training, or aerobics, or a team sport, such as basketball or soccer, girls are getting in on the action. Exercise gets your blood flowing and sets your mind on fire. It can give you energy and make you feel strong and capable.

The popularity of the WNBA and the championship U.S. women's soccer team shows that even at the professional level, sports are not just a man's game. Girls who play sports have confidence, and this is probably because they feel more in control of their bodies. They know how to go fast and how to take chances. Done with a healthy spirit of fun and competition, exercise can help you feel your best.

The Meditative Arts

Practicing meditative arts is another way to help our bodies and minds to grow healthier. Have you ever stopped to look at waves crashing on the beach, a candle flame, or even a tree in the park and felt as if you were lost in the image, as if you were entering a trance? You may not have realized it,

71

but in a way, you were meditating at that moment. Visual artists, writers, musicians, and dancers get so involved in their art that they experience a form of meditation while they are engaged in creating. Meditation is really just focusing intently on one sound, idea, image, or goal.

Our society moves at a fast pace, with e-mail, cell phones, and television as our constant companions. Practicing meditation is a way to prevent your world from spinning out of control. It's like going on vacation in your mind even when your body is stuck on the bus or in your room. A regular meditation practice will bring tremendous rewards. Do you ever have trouble concentrating on homework or simply reading a book? Do you feel as if you sometimes have to read the same paragraph over and over again? Meditation will bring you an inner peace that will help you master concentration. When you slow down to meditate once a day, or maybe a few times a week, the stuff that used to take forever will come more easily to you.

Meditation will also help you sleep better. If you meditate for a few minutes before you go to bed, you will wake up less tired and more refreshed. When your alarm clock rings or your mom yells at you to get out of bed, you will open your eyes ready to take on any challenge. You will also remember your dreams better.

Meditation: The Basics

So how do we begin? The first task is to choose a mantra. A mantra is simply a sound, word, or phrase that is repeated over and over as you meditate. It can be spoken aloud as a chant or repeated silently to oneself in meditation. A lot of people think the best mantras are the ones that have no clear meaning, the ones that are just sounds. This is so the meditator will not get involved in thinking about meditation. This may sound a little confusing, but the point of meditation is to go beyond, or underneath, thought. You master the mind by controlling the mind. The Catholic form of meditation, saying the rosary, is one kind of mantra. Because I am Jewish, I use a Hebrew prayer, "Ribbono Shel Olam," when I meditate. It means "All One Source." Because Hebrew is not my first language, the phrase feels like more of a sound than an idea. You can choose whatever mantra you want. You can even repeat the word "love" over and over.

If you don't have any ideas for a mantra, I suggest using "hamza." It works with the breath. You say "ham" (huh-AH-m) on the inhalation and "za" on the exhalation. (A hamza is a symbol in the Arabic alphabet that is said to protect people. It looks like an opened palm.)

The first thing you need to do is find a safe, quiet space in which to meditate. Never meditate in bed because sleeping and meditating are two separate activities, although meditation can sometimes make you fall asleep. You can light some incense or a scented candle if you want to.

Some people like to use a meditation cushion to sit on. It's not necessary, but you might want to sit on a pillow to make you more comfortable. Rest your rear end on the edge of the pillow, and let your knees fall open as wide as possible. Roll your shoulders back and straighten out your back. Sit cross-legged. You can even sit against the wall or in a chair if you want back support.

Close your eyes. Breathe naturally. Try to sit for a minute or two before you begin repeating your mantra to slow down the breath and heart rate. Bring your attention to your breath. Do this gently, without force. Then begin to silently repeat "ham" on the inhale and "za" on the exhale, or whatever your chosen mantra is.

Let yourself melt into the process. Thoughts, even obsessive thoughts, are likely to come. Try to let them come and go without attachment. Imagine your thoughts dancing across the movie screen of your mind. But pretend that it really is a movie. Pretend that all the worries and fears that control you are someone else's movie. Note the thoughts, and don't try to control them. When you realize you are thinking thoughts, gently move back into your mantra. This might happen every few seconds. Do not become frustrated. It's perfectly normal. Meditation is an art that takes lots of practice. It will liberate you eventually. Just give it time.

Some meditation teachers suggest that one should meditate for at least twenty minutes per session. That is a good goal, but if you feel you can do it for only five or ten minutes at first, that's okay, too. You can work your way up to longer periods of meditation. You may find yourself in a deep state of relaxation, or you may not. You also may feel nothing at first because you are still so attached to your thoughts. When you're finished meditating, sit for a moment or two until you come back to normal awareness. Don't get up too fast. It is okay to glance at a clock if you are timing your meditation. But don't use an alarm clock to shock you out of your altered state. There are different opinions regarding the best time to meditate. Before breakfast in the morning and before dinner in the evening are good times. Digestion is known to shut down during meditation, so it's a good idea to have an empty stomach.

The most important part of meditation is showing up. Having the intention to meditate is more important than getting it "right." There is no right. You might fall asleep, or obsess, or try to plan your science project during meditation. Allow it to happen. Just gently go back to the mantra. You will see results. Just be patient. A regular meditation practice is deeply rewarding. It will help reveal your true beauty.

Look Around

You can also try out any of the Eastern movement arts, like yoga, t'ai chi, or qi gong (pronounced chi gung). Movement can create a stillness in the mind. These arts exploded in popularity in the last few years, with good reason: Regular practice can provide you with a lithe and healthy body. They increase strength and stamina, and the discipline a regular practice requires can teach you a lot about your life.

Turning Attitude into Action

Gloria Steinem, one of the early leaders of the second wave of feminism, which arose in the 1960s and 1970s, coined a phrase that has stuck with us for decades. She said, "The personal is the political." That's really what the foundation of this book is all about. What do you think it means?

We're taught in history class that politics is something removed from our lives. There is a system of checks and balances, of government, of policy, but really we're not meant to get involved in it unless we want to run for office. Writing a letter to a senator is a way we might consider to try to effect change, but few people even try to do this. There are activists on all sides of the political spectrum, right and left, Republican and Democrat and Libertarian, who are involved in the political process. But you might not think that has anything to do with you. And there's a good chance that you don't really care. It might bore you to tears.

That's because it's hard to get passionate about stuff that doesn't seem to have anything to do with our lives. Even if you're a really good person who becomes concerned when you hear about starving children, taking action to change lives probably means less to you than getting your homework done. There's nothing wrong with that. The news can feel like fiction to us. In fact, it's meant to. That way, we will stay out of the political process. The corporate news is not meant to call us to action. It's meant to keep us sitting on our sofas transfixed so that we stay tuned during the commercials, which are actually louder than the program that we're watching to get our attention. So why get passionate about anything?

Think about what moves you. Did you cry as you wrote entries in your journal while journeying through this book? Your own issues are something to get passionate about. You understand them. They speak to you. You are learning how to survive in the world by exploring the jungle of your psyche. How does this relate to politics?

When Steinem coined that phrase, it was because of a personal journey she had gone on herself. When women all over the country read *The Feminine Mystique*, they not only woke up individually but had a collective uprising into consciousness. Betty Friedan, author of *Mystique*, went on to found the National Organization for Women, also known as NOW. They saw that a system of politics, of patriarchy, was controlling their personal lives. Their relationships with their husbands and children were molded by society's expectation that they would stay home and not have a career. And they chose to change that.

Another powerful example of how the personal continues to be the political even today is the topic of abortion. Before the *Roe v. Wade* decision in 1973, women who wanted to terminate a pregnancy had to have the termination procedure done illegally. Thousands of women died or were terribly wounded during these operations, which were often done by unqualified people or without anesthetic. When the Supreme Court made the decision to legalize abortion, it had a profound effect on the personal lives of women.

What's Next?

What does this mean for you today? The beauty myth and its effect on our bodies and minds are strong examples of the personal/political relationship. We went over this in the first few chapters. When self-hatred imposed by media images causes eating disorders, the personal is very political in a very dangerous way. How can we change ourselves to change the world?

Take a few minutes to look at some of the things you've learned about yourself by reading this book. Think about the wounds that have been revealed to you and begun to heal. How are they political wounds? Trace them back to the source. If much of what you've discovered about your beauty wounds comes from your family relationships, try to look at where it all started. Write in your journal about how the personal is the political in your own life.

You've begun the process of understanding and deconstructing images and messy messages offered by the world around you. You're on your way to not letting fashion magazines get you down. When you witness too-skinny women on television, you know why they look that way. You are learning not to be angry and jealous of strangers. You are learning to look at them as your sisters, girls and women in the same boat as you. You are beginning to know the motivations of your mom and dad. Perhaps you've realized that this journey is too deep to explore on your own, and you've sought therapy to get you through the maze. You are getting stronger, learning to love yourself, and sharing your new power with your friends. Maybe you've got it together on one of the above, but the rest are still a mess. You will get there, I promise. Even if the changes hurt, they will help you grow.

Wherever you are on the continuum of healing, it can help you get there faster and better if you share your wisdom with the world. It makes sense that the first people you would want to spread the word to would be other girls, right? Maybe your friends first. If you know someone with an eating disorder, perhaps you can point her in the right direction now. That is a political act. Helping a friend get through struggling with body image might seem like an isolated act of compassion, but the truth is you'll learn more about yourself, and you'll be helping your friend get strong enough to help the next girl who suffers. No compassionate act ever really stands alone. Your wisdom will be passed on and on.

Many therapists say they went into the field because they were mired in their own pain. The only way they could see their way through was to help others. Paulo Freire was a South American teacher/activist who died in 1997 after a lifetime of dedication to social change based on compassion. He said, "Authentic help means that all who are involved help each other mutually, growing together in the common effort to understand the reality which they seek to transform. Only through such praxis [action]—when those who help and those who are being helped help each other simultaneously—can the act of helping become free from the distortion in which the helper dominates the helped."

I couldn't have written this book unless I knew what it felt like to get stuck in the mirror. I see you, dear reader, as a sister. And I don't see myself as a leader. I'm someone who felt the tremendous weight of the "iron maiden" and survived. We all exist here together, and writing this book has been a healing journey for me. So you've helped me by being my reader. It's a mutual exchange, like Freire suggested. Naomi Wolf, author of *The Beauty Myth*, has exchanged this kind of healing energy with women all over the world since she published her book. But you certainly don't have to be an author to become a part of the dynamic. You already are.

Since your knowledge has transformed you, what can you do to help? What about starting a beauty standard discussion group in your school? If you can round up a bunch of girls who are into raising the roof and discovering the power of the personal in the political, you might get a great discussion group going. You can scour the Internet for body image discussion boards and post your own thoughts. You can check the back of this book for a site directing you to many such Web sites. You can read, read, read. And write, write, write. Publish an editorial in your school newspaper. Write letters to the editors of local and national newspapers. Write to fashion magazines and tell them what you really think about their ads. Boycott magazines that don't cater to real girls. Don't forget to share your mission. You are paving the way for the next wave of empowered girls, maybe even helping to create a world without distorting images.

Grrrl Style

We've briefly explored the history of feminism. Now we'll take a look at what girls like you are doing right now to make a difference and how you can add your voice to the mix. Finally, after what seems a thousand years of agitation, girls' and women's voices get heard. We imagine, create, and publish ideas that stimulate change. Women continue to constantly do battle with forces of institutionalized misogyny (hatred and fear of women) in our culture. But we've got a plan now, and it's a little easier to make change because a trail has been blazed by sisters and mothers who had it harder than we did. Fighting your own inner battle with the beauty myth is the first step to becoming a trailblazer yourself. Once you make your discoveries about how to love yourself, you can share your wisdom and become a part of the solution.

If you gain the strength to stop comparing yourself to images constructed by the media, you will be a step closer to being unafraid to claim your power. For me, the moment I took ownership of the word "feminist" was a kind of birth. I knew that it had an ugly connotation, but even the ugliness of it gave it an appeal that I sought. I knew that announcing myself as a feminist in circles beyond the comfort of women's studies classes would be met with raised eyebrows and snickers. I learned to invite the skepticism. It gave me an opportunity to speak out and inform those not in the know about the true meaning of feminism. I learned to give brief history lessons to the uninitiated, both men and women, without getting on a soapbox.

Many women, even intelligent and educated ones, continue to fear the label "feminist." They still believe being a feminist means that you are a man-hater and a butch (this is a slur used to describe masculine-looking women, but one that has been appropriated by the lesbian community) and that you're angry all the time. Rush Limbaugh, a conservative commentator, coined the term "femi-nazi" a few years ago. These notions are nonsense. Declaring yourself a feminist means that you have observed the world and your place in it and that you recognize that women are not getting what they deserve. There are plenty of guys who are proud to call themselves feminists. And not just to pick up cool girls! It means that you believe that work still needs to be done and that you're not afraid to stand up for it. If you want to stand up in high heels and evening gowns, you can still be a feminist. If you want to shave your head, you can be a feminist. All it requires is commitment.

Take a moment to write about your associations with the word "feminist." What does it mean to you? How do you feel about telling others, especially ones that don't like feminists, that you are proud to be one?

Riding the Third Wave

Feminism is a lot different than it was even twenty years ago. In the early 1990s, some pundits declared that we were living in the "postfeminist" era. They announced that feminism was over. Active feminists found this declaration rather curious because they were still forging new territory. Some of the staunchest opponents of feminism are women. It would probably take a deep probing to understand exactly why some women continue to discredit their sisters.

Girls like you are making change every day in their schools, at their computers, on stage, and in their homes. Understanding who you are is the first step. When we share our understanding with our sisters, we are activists.

Since the early 1990s, feminism has taken on new and dynamic forms. By now you've certainly heard of the term "girl power." But be careful not to confuse true girl power with the media's marketing creations. For example, even if you liked the style and music of the Spice Girls, they have watered down the idea of girl power and made it into a marketing ploy. They wanted you to buy more records, not to realize your true power. The women artists making music in your best interest tend not to get the biggest deals. A good example of this is Kathleen Hanna of the band Bikini Kill. This band grew out of the male-dominated punk scene. She was one of the founders of the "Riot Grrl" movement, which spun into a new and powerful tool for girls to express themselves and claim their power. Ani DiFranco is another musical trailblazer. She has been making folk-punk music about the real issues in women's lives for years now. More recently, there has been the Lilith Fair phenomenon, which eventually became part of the mainstream.

The Guerrilla Girls are a group of women artists who are sick and tired of the male-dominated art scene in New York City. Sporting furry gorilla masks, they once took to the streets and made art into activism. They did not leave their sense of humor at home, either. They made posters with slogans like this: "Q: Do women need to be naked to get into the Metropolitan Museum? A: Less than 5 percent of the artists in the museum are women, but 85 percent of the nudes are female." The Guerrilla Girls show us how important it is to merge art and activism. Their work makes it seem as if making noise about issues and making art are meant for each other.

Zines

Creativity is one key to growth. Zines are one of the major forces of DIY (do-it-yourself) media: The creation of independent, self-made zines has, in a large way, been a response to the monolithic message of the corporate world. Girls (and boys) woke up and said, "What about what I think?" They realized that the magazines they saw on the shelves did not represent their views. Because of advances in desktop publishing, it's relatively easy to achieve a cheap, fast dissemination of ideas. In the beginning, most zines were print only—they were stapled together and left at local book and record stores.

The Internet makes it possible for zine makers to reach the entire world, not just their neighborhood. And over the Internet, no paper gets wasted! For a listing of cool e-zines, turn to the back of this book.

The most important contribution you can make to society is to be true to yourself. Even when you get involved with a really cool, cutting-edge group, there still might be ideas that you disagree with. The word "movement" starts with MOVE, and that means that it's your job to keep it in motion. Keep asking questions about who you are and how you fit (or fail to fit) into the world around you. Have compassion for yourself. And remind yourself every day that it's great to be a girl.

Glossary

airbrushing   A technique used by graphic designers to change images in magazines and advertisements; often used to mask imperfections on models' bodies and faces.

anorexia   An eating disorder marked by self-induced starvation.

Aphrodite   The Greek goddess of love and beauty; called Venus by the Romans

appropriation   Taking an idea or description of something thought to be negative and making it into something positive and powerful. (Like girls taking back the word "chick.")

bulimia   An eating disorder marked by self-induced vomiting after eating.

capitalism   The predominant economic and political system of our times, dependent on private capital and profit making.

corset   A type of constrictive clothing worn over the midsection of the body by women of the Victorian era.

feminism   Movement dedicated to women's rights and ending oppression and sexism.

iron maiden   A torture device used during medieval times.
Ishtar   An Egyptian goddess.
Isis   An Egyptian goddess.
Kali   A Hindu goddess symbolizing power.
Madonna/whore complex   A psychological term applied
   when men believe that women fit only two stereotypes—the virginal, chaste type or the slutty type.
misogyny   The fear and hatred of women.
monotheism   The belief in one god.
paganism   The belief in many gods.
patriarchy   A term used to describe a system marked by
   a division of power that favors men.
Plato   A Greek philosopher.
suffragists   People who support women's right to vote.
Venus   A Roman goddess, known as Aphrodite to
   the Greeks.
Victorian era   The era when Queen Victoria ruled; a
   time generally regarded as having prudish and strict
   social values.

Where to Go
for Help

In the United States

About-Face
About-Face promotes positive self-esteem in girls and women of all ages, sizes, races, and backgrounds through a spirited approach to media education, outreach, and activism.
Web site: http://about-face.org

Girls Incorporated
120 Wall Street, 3rd Floor
New York, NY 10005
(800) 374-4475
Web site: http://www.girlsinc.org

International Size Acceptance Association
P.O. Box 82126
Austin, TX 78758

National Eating Disorders Association
603 Stewart Street, Suite 803
Seattle, WA 98101
(206) 382-3587
Web site: http://www.nationaleatingdisorders.org

National Women's Health Network
514 10th Street NW, Suite 400
Washington, DC 20004
(202) 347-1140
Web site: http://www.womenshealthnetwork.org

Overeaters Anonymous Headquarters
World Service Office
P.O. Box 44020,
Rio Rancho, NM 87124-4020
(505) 891-2664
Web site: http://www.overeatersanonymous.org

Rape, Abuse, and Incest National Network (RAINN)
635-B Pennsylvania Avenue SE
Washington, DC 20003
(800) 656-HOPE (4673)
e-mail: RAINNmail@aol.com
Web site: http://www.rainn.org

SAFE (Self Abuse Finally Ends)
Linden Oaks Hospital
852 West Street
Naperville, IL 60540
(800) DONT CUT (366-8288)
Web site: http://www.selfinjury.com

Sexuality Information and Education Council of the
    United States (SIECUS)
130 West 42nd Street, Suite 350
New York, NY 10036
(212) 819-9770
e-mail: siecus@siecus.org
Web site: http://www.siecus.org

Violence Against Women Office
801 7th Street NW
Washington, DC 20531
(202) 307-6026
Web site: http://www.ojp.usdoj.gov/vawo

In Canada

Kids Help Foundation
National Office
439 University Avenue, Suite 300
Toronto, ON M5G 1Y8
(416) 586-5437

Kids Help Phone
(800) 668-6868
Web site: http://kidshelp.sympatico.ca

Lambton Health Unit
Youth Issues
e-mail: lambhlth@ebtech.net
Web site: http://www.lambtonhealth.on.ca/
    youth/index.asp

Planned Parenthood Federation of Canada
1 Nicholas Street, Suite 430
Ottawa, ON K1N 7B7
(613) 241-4474
e-mail: admin@ppfc.ca
Web site: http://www.ppfc.ca

Sexuality Education Resource Centre
Winnipeg Office
555 Broadway Avenue, 2nd Floor
Winnepeg, MB R3C 0W4
(204) 982-7800
Web site: http://www.serc.mb.ca

Web Sites

Due to the changing nature of Internet links, the Rosen
Publishing Group, Inc., has developed an online list of
Web sites related to the subject of this book. This site is
updated regularly. Please use this link to access the list:

http://www.rosenlinks.com/cop/beau/

For Further Reading

Books

Brittenum, Lonnice. *Kitchen Beautician: For Colored Girls Who Dissed the Beauty Standard When It Became Too Rough.* New York: Three Rivers Press, 1997.

Brumberg, Joan Jacobs. *The Body Project: An Intimate History of American Girls.* New York: Random House, 1997.

Carroll, Rebecca. *Sugar in the Raw: Voices of Young Black Girls in America.* New York: Three Rivers Press, 1997.

Edut, Ophira, ed. *Adios, Barbie: Young Women Write About Body Image and Identity.* Seattle, WA: Seal Press, 1998.

Edut, Ophira, and Rebecca Walker, eds. *Body Outlaws: Young Women Write About Body Image and Identity.* Seattle, WA: Seal Press, 2000.

Friedan, Betty. *The Feminine Mystique.* New York: W.W. Norton, 1963.

Gray, Heather M., and Samantha Phillips. *Real Girl, Real World: Tools for Finding Your True Self.* Seattle, WA: Seal Press, 1998.

Green, Karen, and Tristan Taormino, eds. *A Girl's Guide to Taking Over the World: Writings from the Girl Zine Revolution.* New York: St. Martin's Press, 1997.

Halprin, Sara. *Look at My Ugly Face: Myths and Musings on Beauty and Other Perilous Obsessions with Women's Appearance*. New York: Viking, 1995.

Johnston, Joni E. *Appearance Obsession: Learning to Love the Way You Look*. Deerfield Beach, FL: Health Communications, 1993.

Karp, Marcelle, and Debbie Stoller. *The Bust Guide to the New Girl Order*. New York: Penguin Books, 1999.

Pipher, Mary. *Reviving Ophelia: Saving the Selves of Adolescent Girls*. New York: Ballantine Books, 1994.

Thompson, Becky. *A Hunger So Wide and So Deep: A Multiracial View of Women's Eating Problems*. Minneapolis, MN: University of Minnesota Press, 1997.

Vanzant, Iyanla. *Don't Give It Away*. New York: Simon & Schuster, 1999.

Wolf, Naomi. *The Beauty Myth: How Images of Beauty Are Used Against Women*. New York: Anchor Doubleday, 1991.

Magazines

BlueJean
Web site: http://www.bluejeanonline.com

Ms.
Web site: http://www.msmagazine.com

New Moon for Girls
Web site: http://www.newmoon.org

Index

About the Author

Stefanie Iris Weiss is a freelance writer, a professor of writing, and the author of four other books for young adults. She lives in New York City. Contact her at: stefanie_iris@yahoo.com.

Acknowledgments

To all my loved ones: Mom, Dad, Hal, Liz, Sherene, Rachelle, Ora, Missy, Jodi, Zig, Lynn, Jaimie, Gabby, and Joshua. Your kindness is boundless and true. Thank you for your inspiration.

Thanks to my students, past, present, and future. To the wise ones: Malcolm X, Martin Luther King Jr., Emma Goldman, the Goddess in all of her names, bell hooks, Paulo Freire, Marge Piercy, Ellen Turk, Naomi Wolf, Marion Woodman, and other teachers too numerous to name.

Finally, to all of the women and girls who witness the world from within their sacred bodies and know that their beauty radiates from an even deeper place. We wrote this book together.